BRAIN BOOSTERS

PLANET EARTH PUZZLES

by
Vicky Barker
& Ste Johnson

LiTTle GENiUS BOOKs

Published by Little Genius Books. www.littlegeniusbooks.com. • 10 9 8 7 6 5 4 3 2 1 • 9781953344625

Text and illustrations copyright © 2021 b small publishing ltd. Art Director: Vicky Barker. Editorial: Sam Hutchinson. Printed in China by WKT Co. Ltd.

Which climber will reach the summit first?

A

B

C

DID YOU KNOW?

Although it's the highest peak above sea level, Everest is not the tallest mountain on Earth. Mauna Kea is the tallest, but it is mostly under water.

Can you copy this thunderstorm picture in the grid below?

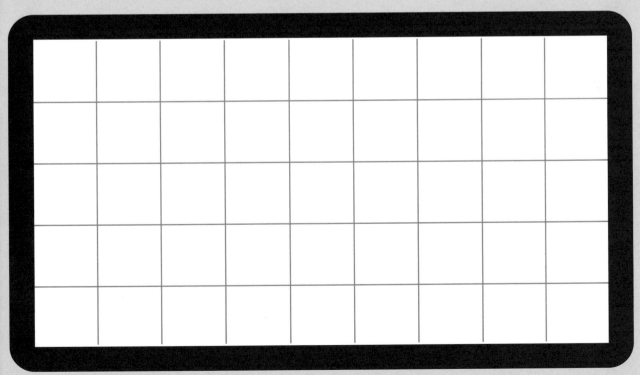

Dig into this Planet Earth word search.

```
F Y D I V E R S V O X Y G E N K
C O N T I N E N T E U S X T M C
S S Q M P E Q U A T O R U U A I
L I O R A R H M P F D O S R T N
H A L A I G J H A L C A E T M O
R R F I V D M B L E A X A L O T
I F E N D S L A A H X T W E S C
V I E F X L L N D R R C E M P E
E S R O C K Y X P O A X E S H T
R H P R S K M M T V L X D H E M
F D S E O W A N R L O U Q W R A
B U B S L E N X E X P L X U E R
E L G T J F T N S M U K C L L C
R Q U A K E L S E E S K L A S M
O A L S E A E R D F L L V H N P
C B A C R U S T E A X A B A R O
```

ROCK	**VOLCANO**	**DESERT**	**LAVA**
OCEAN	**TECTONIC**	**RAINFOREST**	**MAGMA**
CORE	**CONTINENT**	**POLAR**	**RIVER**
ATMOSPHERE	**OIL**	**MANTLE**	**QUAKE**
EQUATOR	**PLATES**	**CRUST**	**OXYGEN**

Can you spot ten differences in these scenes?

DID YOU KNOW? Cherry blossoms are Japan's national flower. They can be pink, white, yellow or green and they stand for renewal and hope.

Which group of islands is this sailor exploring?

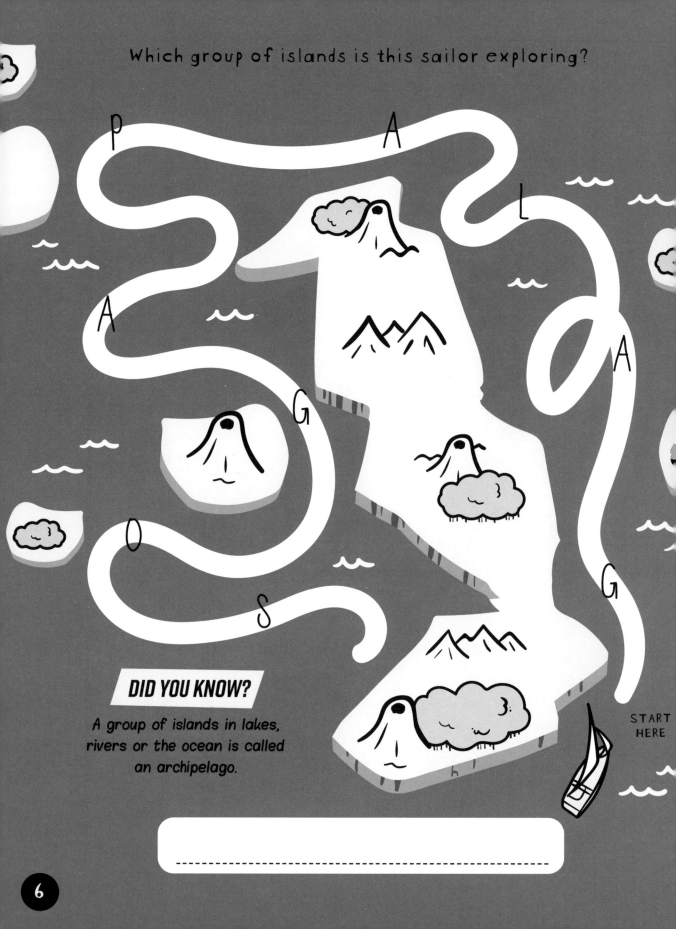

DID YOU KNOW?

A group of islands in lakes, rivers or the ocean is called an archipelago.

Is there an odd or even number of snowflakes below? Count them and find out!

DID YOU KNOW?

Snowflakes are mostly unique but not always. Identical snowflakes were found by American scientist Nancy Knight in 1988.

Go diving in the Great Barrier Reef! What can you see?

DID YOU KNOW? Coral reefs are very delicate ecosystems, sensitive to temperature changes and the impact of human behavior.

8

Fill in the blank hexagons by adding together the two numbers below.

5   7   9   12

65

10   2   15   11

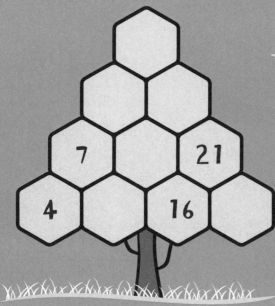

7   21
4   16

15
6   1   17

DID YOU KNOW?

The world's largest living tree is called General Sherman and lives in Sequoia National Park, California.

Help this explorer safely back to base during the polar night. Watch out for rocks, wolves and polar bears!

DID YOU KNOW?

The polar night is when it stays dark outside for twenty-four hours a day. This occurs only inside the Arctic and Antarctic Circles.

Each of these sets of differently shaped clouds has its own number pattern. Can you work them out and fill in the blanks?

Find the odd one out in each row.

Match these landforms to their shadows.

True or false?

1. The Sahara desert is wider than the USA.

2. The water on Earth is 97% salt water.

3. In the rainforest, rain can take 10 minutes to reach the ground.

4. The lowest ever temperature recorded in Antarctica was −89.4 degrees Celcius.

5. The Indian Ocean is the coldest ocean.

6. The higher up in the atmosphere you go, the thicker the air gets.

Color in the layers of atmosphere. Cover the page and try to remember the correct order.

OUTER SPACE

International Space Station

Highest parachute jump

16

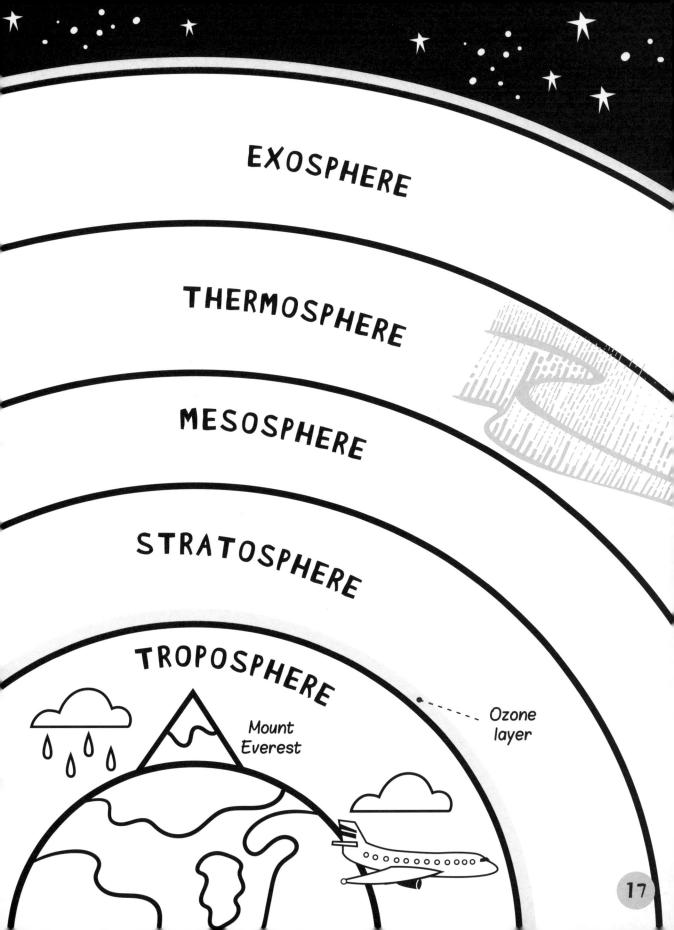

EXOSPHERE

THERMOSPHERE

MESOSPHERE

STRATOSPHERE

TROPOSPHERE

Mount
Everest

Ozone
layer

17

Can you complete this journey to the center of the Earth?

START

END

Use this step-by-step guide to draw an Easter Island head!

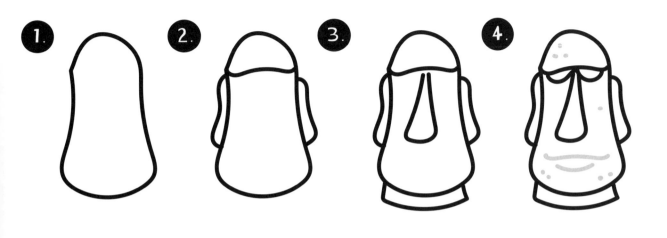

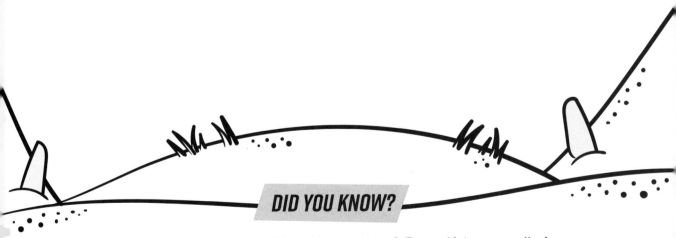

DID YOU KNOW?

These Moai were carved by the people of Rapa Nui, now called
Easter Island, over 500 years ago. They are carved from volcanic ash.

Find the group of weather symbols that matches the one on the right.

20

Connect the dots to reveal what's hiding in the rainforest.

DID YOU KNOW?

In one square mile of rainforest, you can find around 100 different species of tree.

21

Can you help this person out of the vast, hot desert?

START HERE

DID YOU KNOW? Deserts are not always hot and sandy, but they are the driest places on Earth. There are deserts in polar regions too.

Chichen Itza, Mexico

Draw the other half of these great landmarks and color them in.

Taj Mahal, India

Christ the Redeemer, Brazil

Great Sphinx of Giza, Egypt

Help this driver outrun the tornado! Draw a line as fast as you can without going off the sides. Time yourself! Use different colored pens and let your friends try.

DID YOU KNOW? Tornado winds can reach speeds of over 300 miles (483 km) per hour.

24

Can you find the row that matches the silhouette?

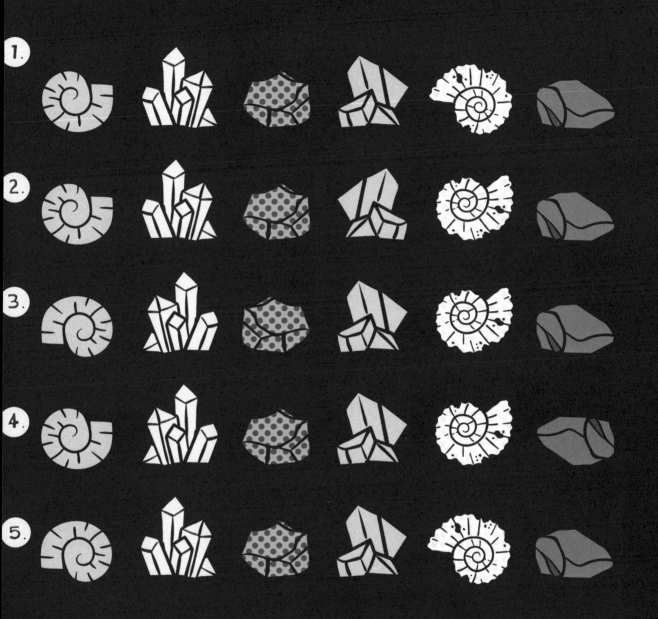

What is the correct sequence here?

1   2   3   4   5

Subtract all the spaces with a dot marked in them by coloring them in. You will reveal a picture in the space left behind!

Are these flowers or bees?

DID YOU KNOW? Bees transport pollen between flowers and crops, helping to produce the fruit and vegetables that humans eat every day.

Can you work out the answers to these sums?

Can you find these squares in the picture below?

Are there more stalactites or stalagmites?
See the fact below for a clue.

DID YOU KNOW?

A stalactite
hangs down and
a stalagmite
stands up.

31

Can you complete this picture grid?
Fill in all of the boxes with one of the four
pictures. Every column, row and four-square
block must contain one of each.

This volcano will erupt if the total of all of the sums added together is more than 100. Work out the sums to find out if you need to draw an explosion!

36 ÷ 3

6 x 4

2 x 9

9 - 7

8 + 8

5 + 2

3 + 7

4 x 3

Something in this snowy scene is out of place.
Can you find what it is?

What can you see when you look at these cloud shapes?
Doodle a cute face on the Sun!

DID YOU KNOW? White clouds fill with water droplets, which reflect less light and make them look grey.

Starting at London and without taking your pen off the page,
follow the letters around until you find each of the
nine capital cities.

START HERE →

L O N D O N P A R I
O H E L S I N R D S
Y N O S L O K I A R
K O B S I L I D M O
O T S N E H T A E M

Add icicles to the branches so that each row
(across, down and diagonal) adds up to 15.

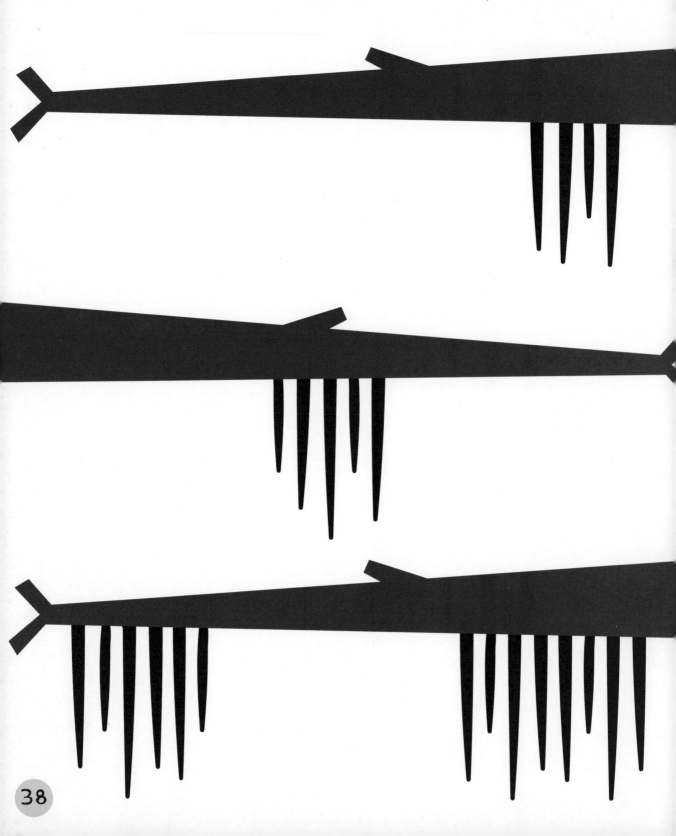

38

1.

_ _ _ _ _

_ _ _ _ _ _ _

H S O T U
I C A R E M A

2.

_ _ _ _ _

_ _ _ _ _ _ _

R H O N T
A C I R A E M

3.

_ _ _ _

I S A A

4.

_ _ _ _ _ _

P U R E O E

5.

_ _ _ _ _ _

F C A R I A

6.

_ _ _ _ _ _ _ _ _ _ _

T L S A A R I A U A S

7.

_ _ _ _ _ _ _ _ _ _

C A T N A R I C T A

QUICK QUIZ!

1. How long does it take the light from the Sun to reach Earth?

   a) 2 seconds b) 8 minutes

   c) 1 hour d) 1 day

2. What percentage of the Earth is covered in water?

   a) About 50% b) About 30%

   c) About 70% d) About 60%

3. The volcanoes around the edges of the Pacific Ocean are known as ... ?

   a) Ring of Fire b) Circle of Flame

   c) House of Lava d) Crown of Eruptions

4. The inner core of the Earth is made of?

   a) Solid metal b) Magma

   c) Soil d) Candyfloss

5. The continents on our planet used to be one giant slab of land called ...

   a) Tangaea b) Bangaea c) Mangaea d) Pangaea

Can you draw all the colors of
a beautiful sunset?

This diver wants to photograph a very specific fish. Follow the instructions to find out which one.

Cross out:
- Even numbers
- Numbers starting with 2
- The number of days in the week
- The number of oceans
- The number of points on 5 triangles

Can you spot ten differences in these scenes?

Nearly two million animals of different types migrate in a clockwise direction around the Serengeti every year, searching for food.

Can you break this code to
reveal the picture?
Color in each of the squares
in this list to see what is hidden.

A - 14, 15, 16
B - 6, 7, 8, 13, 14, 16
C - 2, 6, 8, 11, 12, 16
D - 6, 8, 10, 16
E - 3, 5, 6, 9, 13, 14, 15,
    16, 18
F - 4, 11, 13
G - 4, 13, 14, 15
H - 5, 8, 16
I - 6, 11, 14, 15, 16
J - 2, 7, 13
K - 4, 8, 12

L - 9, 11, 16
M - 8, 9, 10, 11, 12
N - 7, 9, 13
O - 6, 10, 14
P - 5, 9, 15
Q - 4, 8, 16
R - 3, 17
S - 2, 3, 4, 5, 6, 7, 8, 9, 10, 11,
    12, 13, 14, 15, 16, 17, 18
T - 1, 2, 3, 4, 5, 6, 7, 8, 9, 10, 11,
    12, 13, 14, 15, 16, 17, 18

Answers

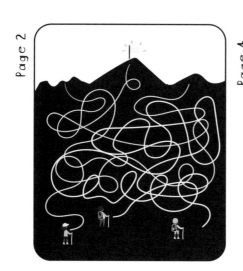

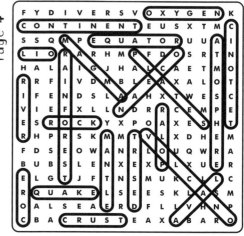

Page 6
GALAPAGOS

Page 7 ODD
There are 31 snowflakes.

Page 9

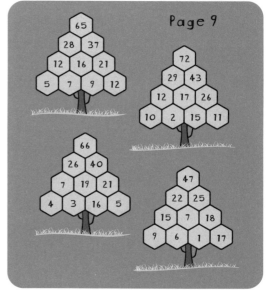

Page 10

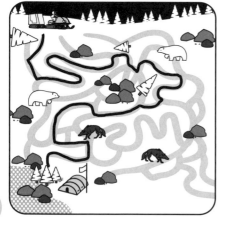

Page 11

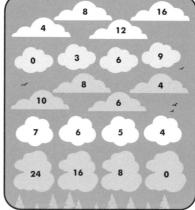

Page 12

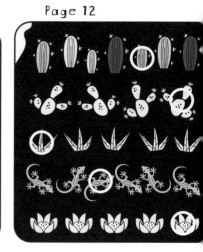

Page 13

Page 14

Page 15

1. True
2. True
3. True
4. True
5. False
6. False

Page 18

Page 20

Page 21

Page 22

Page 25   ROW 4

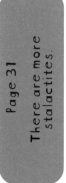

Page 26

1. E   2. C   3. A   4. D   5. B

Page 27

Page 29

Page 30

Page 31

There are more stalactites.

Page 32

Page 33

101!

Page 34

47

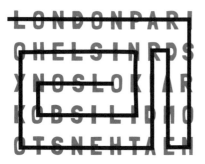

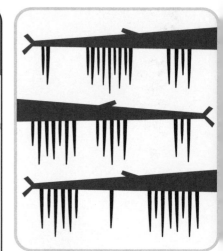

Page 39

1. NORTH AMERICA
2. SOUTH AMERICA
3. ASIA
4. EUROPE
5. AFRICA
6. AUSTRALASIA
7. ANTARCTICA

Page 40

1. b
2. c
3. c
4. a
5. d

Page 42

Page 43

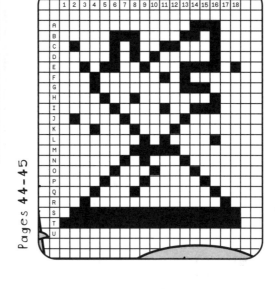